Splendid Signature:

Rhythmic Strokes of a Quill

Splendid Signature:
Rhythmic Strokes of a Quill

Malakshmi Borthakur

Introduction by
Anand Prakash

BLACK EAGLE BOOKS
Dublin, USA | BBSR, India

Black Eagle Books
USA address:
7464 Wisdom Lane
Dublin, OH 43016

India address:
E/312, Trident Galaxy, Kalinga Nagar,
Bhubaneswar-751003, Odisha, India

E-mail: info@blackeaglebooks.org
Website: www.blackeaglebooks.org

First International Edition Published by
Black Eagle Books, 2022

SPLENDID SIGNATURE: RHYTHMIC STROKES OF A QUILL
by **Malakshmi Borthakur**

Copyright © Malakshmi Borthakur

Cover & Interior Design: Ezy's Publication

ISBN- 978-1-64560-088-6 (Paperback)
Library of Congress Control Number: 2022950397

Printed in the United States of America

in the invisible hands
of
my father
Sarat Chandra Borthakur

Book with a Shining Tomorrow

Anand Prakash

The present book of poems titled *Splendid Signature: Rhythmic Strokes of a Quill* falls under the category of women's writing, a distinct presence in the cultural domain today. It tells us about the problems women face with respect to their right of equality, dignity and independence. In their case, motherhood is not the only issue, the family and traditional norms are not the only concerns. There are aspects stretching to the larger social expanse that exerts its influence at subtle as well as unsubtle levels. Expressing oneself poetically is a task of its own kind. One runs into the many ideological and value-related hurdles, making the scene problematic if not threatening.

While reading the poems of Malakshmi Borthakur in this volume, one is struck by their simplicity and directness. The words therein denote a message of deep questioning. The outlook working behind the poems seldom comes in the way of communication. It relates to the reader concretely and tellingly, making her/ him feel that all is not right with the world. Yet, there is expression of fulfillment at a few places in the same life-conditions that prevail. As such, the poetic utterances emphasize hope and positive intervention. Note for instance the mental state captured in the following lines:

The cool breeze blowing is making me shiver.
The shawl I'm wearing is unable to give me comfort
Like the passionate moon, I'm also waiting
Like the moon, I'm also in love.

The mention of love is made here as a common reference. In it, the modernist self-consciousness is missing. Loneliness and mechanical living are not the issues. We see instead an assertion. Mark in the context that the moon is passionate and "I am also in love." The use of an apparent cliché to announce one's own standpoint is soft and easy in tone. However, there is suggestion of a dramatic shift when we consider the title under which these lines are placed - "The Pseudonym of Love." We are indeed left to wonder as to what "pseudonym" signifies.

The next poem "I am a Mother" could do without the rhyming but the reader's eye is soon caught by the unconventional biological details of conceiving and delivering a child. Again, the aforementioned simplicity takes over and presents a woman of substance, one who assumes a materialist posture and points towards the need to define oneself. The poet has become the typical female of the human species underlining the fact - "hardship of pregnancy is not a bliss." We are led from thereon to another poem "Bleeding Goddess: An Eternal Love Story" and observe that the scope of the woman's experience has widened to include a whole mythic phenomenon.

Let us not lose sight of the fact that Malakshmi Borthakur is relatively a beginner, the present volume being her first collection. It goes to her credit, therefore, that her concerns consist of grasping the contentious truths of culture, ideology and the folk tale. With help from these, she aims to build an account of a distinct creativity. We might locate in her poems a form of feminism taking shape even as the individual mind grapples with nuances of a complex living. Would poetry assist her in the venture of meaningful existence? The issue is highlighted at length in the volume.

The book has 50 poems that cover a diversity of subjects ranging from individuality, love, and mythology to economic deprivation, childhood, and social violence. At one place, Borthakur expects the reader to think about conditions in which the children of the poor live. The reader confronts them in the lines that follow:

Where will you meet them?
You needn't go far.
Just look around
You can see them anywhere
Working in collieries,
Making bricks in fire kilns,
Cleaning dishes in hotels,
Picking garbage up,
Working in breweries even.
…Without knowing what a childhood literally is
[As] they step into adulthood.

Soon in the poem, hunger becomes a person with a voice that intersects between the abstract and real, casting critical glances at what the humans created in the name of institution and structures. The poet makes Hunger express itself in the first person:

[Bin] is my home after all!
I have full right to go there!
Since birth I've been living there!

That broken bin is
My sweet home,
My only shelter. ("Hunger")

Is there a way out in the middle of such conditions? This question is quietly raised but no specific answer is provided. The silence it causes becomes a comment on the perspective we chose to be guided by in the past.

The theme of love is dealt with in poems such as "Lover's Soliloquy," "My Ideal Moon," "The Gift of Love," to name a few. In these, we come across phrases of the kind, "love remains fallen, uncared," "fresh Jasmine adding on my tomb," and "[The Woman] frozen as ice," as well as "floating like icebergs/ In the sea of heaven." Note that the images of love in the phrases are of a distinct character not associated with the conventional relationship between a man and woman. There is as much of living in the cited words as there is of dying, and the two combine to present a problematic. The reader is left to imagine the state of love in contemporary surroundings. It appears to be a case of the poet's concern with the travails of the existing norms bearing upon the sensitive sections in our midst. Malakshmi Thakur aims to project the emotions as part of experience she visualizes in contemporary surroundings.

Borthakur dwells a great deal upon questions of culture where poetry is situated. "Culture" compels the poet to look towards myths impinging on the woman's psyche in our midst. Myths are shown in the poems as integral to a woman's life in her concrete circumstance. Borthakur considers gods and goddesses in terms of woman's mental make-up and biology as well as larger nature with which she is intimately linked. For her, myths work in a deeper layer and help the woman subject evolve an ethos different from that of man. She sets the human female as the domain of nature vis-à-vis the male whose chief connect is the consciously constructed society. The nature-society dialectic emerges in the book as a separation, if not an antagonism. Borthakur treats the theme in view of the feelings residing in the broader 'regional' psyche. To her, the female and male segments stand defined as running parallel to each other, seldom intersecting. The sole point of intersection is in language where nature and society preserve their character.

Significantly, Borthakur refers to social distortions, too, blocking the path of the free woman. The window to freedom in her case is in the form of the love relationship. She idealizes love, presents it as an answer to questions that women in our society face. In this regard, one might interpret love as a dynamic aspect of conducting oneself. Not rooted in institutions and ritualistic conduct, love can be realized by women and men on the move, away from manners to which the two are sought to be tied. For the stranglehold of custom, love may prove to be a recipe. It would rescue the human being from the malaise of problems and issues and offer an alternative path. In one poem, Borthakur requests Jesus to be born again so he became a symbol of hope in conditions of siege in our world. Jesus also stands for deep emotion as well as innate virtue. As we read on, we observe that positive words in the book are freedom, dream, wisdom, coffee, and the untold love story. Rhyme falls in the same category stressing connection, harmony, music. One is also struck by the travelogue of love, an imagined account of breaking away from fixed norms.

In view of the diversity of thought present in this volume, one might happily observe that the poems have a vibrant future, and a potentiality of fuller expression to realize. They unsettle the fixity of preferences that our society adopted under specific pressures. A feminist stress on dignity and courage is the need of the hour.

❑

(*Anand Prakash taught English literature in a Delhi University college till retirement in 2007. He has authored books and edited volumes as well as journals in English and Hindi.*)

From the Poet's Lectern

NAMASKAR to all my beloved friends, readers and well-wishers. I am overjoyed to share my first book of poems in English, *Splendid Signature- Rhythmic Strokes of a Quill* with you all and getting goosebumps as well while writing these words. The reason is, I am not a born poet. It's life who had insisted me to scribble periodically and I still don't know when those scribbles had taken the shape of poetry.

Malakshmi: The Multi Lingual Poet

It was the year 2013, when my daughter Ananya was born. Her birth was a complicated delivery. During that period, I was undergoing lots of pain, physically and emotionally. I felt, those pain were gradually killing my enthusiasm for life. I was in a desperate search for healing myself from that mental trauma. So, as a relief system, I took up writing and started scribbling any kind of crazy thoughts that used to run through my mind. The gradual arrival of stability in my life also had brought with it maturity to my ink and in a certain point of time I could convince myself that those scribbles had turned into mature poetry. Thus, poetry became my therapy, the lone strategy of my survival. In the year 2016, I started bringing my poems to public sight through Facebook. Those poems were all written in my native language, Assamese. There were some friends in Facebook, who used to read my poems regularly and sent me honest feedback. There were many non-Assamese friends too, whom I used to periodically explain the meanings of my Assamese poems in English. As they were enjoying those poems, they suggested that I should write poems in English also. I was so fascinated by the suggestion that I started writing in English too. Gradually I started being a multilingual poet who writes in three languages- English, Hindi and Assamese.

The Persona in My Poetry

Many of my poems are written in the first person. My readers may assume those are autobiographical: the life story of the narrator i.e. me. I have used this literary device with an experiment i.e. a blend of Confessional poetry in English and 'Kotha Kobita' in Assamese; which I consider a powerful device to craft a message, to get connected with my readers well.

I would be glad if I get feedback from you all. Your words for my poems would serve as a great source of inspiration and support to all my future endeavours.

Indira Nagar,   Yours truly,
Lucknow - 226016,   **Malakshmi Borthakur**
Uttar Pradesh, India

CONTENT

The Pseudonym of Love   19

I am a Mother   21

The Bleeding Goddess (Part I)   23

The Bleeding Goddess (Part II)   26

They   29

Love's Soliloquy   31

My Ideal Moon   33

The Lonely Church   35

Hunger   37

Journey   41

The Stories   42

The Birds' Story   43

An Unwritten Verse of Forbidden Love   44

An Ideal Wife   47

Being Alone   49

When I Hold My Golden Pen   51

Love Berg   54

Solace   55

A New Relationship   56

Love of a Kind   58

The Burden   60

Wonder Morning   62

The Wiser Woman   63

The Last Letter   65

The Recipe Of Love   67

Problem is Never the End   68

Survived Bird   70

O' Jesus! Please Be Reborn!   71

An Ode To Freedom   73

A Storm And A Maiden Dream   74

I Don't Want To Be Desdemona	76
The Girl Who Has Refused To Be Born!	77
Love Again	80
Imagination	81
She And A Cup Of Cappuccino	82
A Few Words Of False Hope	83
Smile	85
The Mask	86
Symbiosis	87
Unspoken	88
The Gardener	89
The Travelogue Of Love	91
An Ode To You, O' My Dear!	92
So What If You're A Daughter?	93
A Rhyme Of Love	94
The Fear	95
Determination	96
Not In My Name	97
The Task	101
An Untold Love Story	102
Note of Appreciation	105
Short Review	106
Acknowledgement	108

The Pseudonym of Love

It's a wintry full moon night
I'm sitting on the terrace, engrossed in
My own thoughts
A tranquil silence prevails around
My anklets making the only baffling sound!

The moon is sitting quietly on the parapet
Though every passing minute makes him restless
For long he's been waiting for his beloved
The moonshine, his love for life

The cool breeze makes me shiver
Piercing the shawl I wear
Like the passionate moon, I'm waiting too
As I'm also in love !

The wintry wind makes me miss
The warmth of your embrace
Your cosy touch, your cuddles,
The caress of your breath on my cheeks
Your smooches that give life to my quivering lips

Visualizing with her his meeting,
The desperate moon is smiling

Soon their world would be illuminated
His beloved would come to him tiptoed
The shawl of shyness wearing

The pseudonym of love is waiting
For the love of one's life
If it turns endless, it becomes life taking
I've been in love and also, I've been waiting
The moon's long wait for his coy beloved
Would end soon
But mine?
No!
Under the blue-eyed sky, I've to wait for
Many such full moon nights
Till you come and hold me in your arms.

❑

I am a Mother

Hardship of pregnancy is not a bliss,
It's a phase of pain that all moms do kiss.

My story is one of painful struggle,
With painful moments, where I did wriggle.

My womb was cut and carved,
To make my baby breathe and relieved.

HSG, a painful medical process in womb,
Where I had to bear the pain of a bomb!

The doctors declared my womb as barren,
I was desperate and still saw it as heaven!

I allowed it to be cut and adjusted,
To see it with a baby not congested!

Womb cried out many times in pain,
But it did bear all the process for the gain!

Finally, the day came when I was carrying,
I was happy and up in the air flying!

What a complicated pregnancy it was!
But my faith and tolerance made it pass.

I felt the heavenly kick of her at times,
I felt she was within playing games!

Poor mom me, I cried and wailed
So that her birth never failed !

Finally came the day heavenly,
I heard my daughter's first cry and felt queenly!

I became a blessed mother,
Holding her, we cried in happiness together.

❏

The Bleeding Goddess
(An Eternal Love Story)

Part I

Women's menstruation is a natural biological process;
Every woman faces it with much difficulties.

But still in India, people hesitate to speak aloud and
discuss about it in a public domain;
Yet, there's an ancient temple that celebrates this natural
process of menstruation, the 'power within every woman !

Located in India's north eastern region, Assam's Neelachal
Hill in Guwahati City;
The temple is of the deity, revered worldwide as the
'Bleeding Goddess', Kamakhya Devi.

Every year during the month of June, the Bramhaputra
river near the Kamakhya temple turns red for three days !
It is believed that during this period the Goddess
Kamakhya menstruates !

There's a story behind this unique phenomenon;
A story of penance, anguish, loss and pain !

A story that revolves around Lord Shiva or Mahadev and
Goddess Sati;
A story of destruction, atonement rebirth, reunion and
above all 'love exemplary !

Sati was the daughter of Queen Prasuti and king Daksha;
She was a boon to the couple from Lord Brahma.

Since her childhood, she adored Lord Shiva and devoted
to him;
From sage Narada, she loved to hear stories and legends
related to him.

As Sati grew up, equally leaped up her devotion for him;
And she vowed that she would marry none else but only
to him.

However, to win over Shiva, the hermit was not at all an
easy task;
But blind in love as she was, she left the luxuries of her
father's palace !

Walking into the forest, started leading an austere life;
Giving up herself fully to the severe penances to become
Shiva's wife !

She renounced food and water at first, then it was time to
forsake her clothing;
Amidst harsh cold and lashing rains, she kept on
meditating and meditating !

Realising the extent of her love and devotion for him, Lord
Shiva was bound to manifest in front of her;

Her devotion brought him back of his ascetic isolation and
the great ascetic was smitten with love for her.

But king Daksha was not pleased with this proposed
marriage;
A dirty, wild and ill-mannered God as his 'son-in-law
wouldn't at all be acceptable, who used to spend most of
his time with ghost and goblins, in cremation grounds and
ashes !

But the determined and strong-willed Sati married Shiva
against her father's wishes;
And merrily she left for Kailash, her husband's place.

❏

The Bleeding Goddess
(An Eternal Love Story)

Part II

Soon after the marriage, Daksha organized a magnificent
sacrificial ritual and invited all Gods and Goddesses
except Sati and Shiva;
But Sati who was missing her parents, wanted to be the
part of this grand ritual with her husband, Shiva.

Not paying heed to her husband's cautions, she left alone
for her father's kingdom;
She reached the palace only to be insulted by her father
with full freedom !

She couldn't bear the harsh and ill words of king Daksha
for her husband and this humiliation prompted her to leap
into the very sacrificial fire;
She thus killed herself to uphold the honour of her
husband and to turn into ashes her father's pride entire !
Meanwhile, Shiva's anger knew no limits when he learnt
what had happened in that institution;
He hurriedly reached the place and in utter agony started
the 'Dance of Destruction !

Shiva's 'Dance of Destruction or the 'Tandav activated the

negative cosmic energy;
As Shiva - the God of wrath, plucked two locks of his hair
and flung them on the ground in fury!

From those locks arose Shiva's two destructive
incarnations - 'Bhadrakali and 'Veerabhadra;
They went on demolishing everything around their sight
and beheaded king Daksha.

The ceremony of destruction continued the whole night;
And finally, with the coming rays of sunshine, Shiva's
wrath got relented and he restored everything destroyed
in the previous night.

He also forgave Daksha and brought him back to his life;
And replaced Daksha's decapitated head with that of a
goat on the plea of Queen Prasuti, Daksha's wife !

A totally devastated Shiva left the place and roamed
around the universe, carrying on his shoulder the burnt
corpse of Sati;
To get Shiva back to his senses, Lord Vishnu sent his
divine weapon 'Sudarshan Chakra to slice Sati's body !

It's believed that the pieces of Sati's body fell to earth at 51
different locations known as holy places of pilgrimage or
'Shakti Peethas;
Today's Kamakhya Temple is the place where fell Sati's
'genitals !

Surprisingly, in the temple you wouldn't find any image
of the deity or statue of her profound;
Rather you would find a genital-shaped stone, laid deep

inside the cave filled with water from a spring flowed perpetually from underground !

A country where a majority of people still consider menstruation as unholy, disgusting and shameful; Kamakhya temple displays a progressive approach - celebrating womanhood, women's fertility and the menstrual cycle.

❑

(Note : When the last piece of Sati's body fell to the ground, a wretched Shiva returned to his ascetic world and sat for deep and long meditation atop the cold mountain, Kailash. Sati was reborn as 'Parvati, the daughter of the king of the Mountains, Himavat and Menavati. Unlike Daksha, Himavat was an ardent devotee of Lord Shiva. Right from her childhood, Parvati grew only to worship and love Shiva. In due course of time, Himavat solemnised her marriage with Shiva. Thus, the eternal lovers reunited to let the world celebrate the victory of love over hatred)

They

On their small shoulders
They carry a huge burden
The burden of a family
Not one or two but for many
They've to work
A plate full of food
Is their only luxury!

At the age of seven or nine
They behave like a parent half!
They've been asked
They've been taught
Only to work, only to earn!
As so many starving stomachs
And so many hungry eyes
Are waiting at the threshold
For their return!

At their birth, their parents rejoice
As it means two more hands to join them soon,
Two more hands working to earn
Two more breads!

Who're they?
Do you know any of them by name?
No, you don't

They're anonymous
They're uncountable in numbers
Where will you meet them?
You needn't go far!
Just look around
You can see them anywhere
Working in collieries,
Making bricks in fire kilns,
Cleaning dishes in hotels,
Picking garbage up,
Working in breweries even!
How will you get them then!

Without knowing what childhood is
They step into adulthood!
And the same process gets repeated
They become parents
And their children get to learn
Few words in succession
'Hunger', 'poverty', 'work' and 'earn'!
Their hands are tied up
With an invisible rope
Of enormous burden!
Until they feel tired
Unless they fall asleep
Till then the show must go on…

Love's Soliloquy

Sitting on a rock
By a river bank
Wearing a white scarf
Shedding a few teardrops
Here I'm, lamenting
The untimely demise
Of the love that has been between us!

My dove white scarf is wriggling
At the cool summer breeze
So is my heart, quivering!
I can hear it palpitating faster
As the last pinch of ash
Of your memory is going
To be immersed in the water!

I see a pair of migrating birds
Flying towards *Jatinga*!
To give their lives
For the cause of 'love'!
The mountains will resonate
Their loud shrieks!
Ah! How fortunate they're!
Living for love and now dying too
For a pristine cause!

We humans are so unfortunate!
Seldom we listen,

Seldom we pay heed to
What our hearts speak!
We are such shrewd traders!
Like anything, we barter love too!
And if we see
More profit somewhere,
We easily shift!
We don't pamper,
We don't water,
The seed of love in the heart
To grow further!
And love remains fallen, uncared
Like a corpse, unrecognized
In the morgue!

Shall I blame you
For deceiving me?
No! I shall not!
Could I expect you
To be true to me?
No, I couldn't!
You couldn't be hers!
Could you be mine?
No! You couldn't!
How comfortably
We quote Shakespeare,
"Frailty, thy name is woman!"
No! It's time to change this personification
And say,
"Frailty, thy name is 'human'!

❏

**Jatinga - Jatinga, a village on a ridge, is located in Dima Hasao district of Assam state in India, famous for the strange phenomenon of migrating birds' committing 'suicide'.*

My Ideal Moon

Above my terrace, on the blue sky, lives my neighbour,
the moon
He smiles at me with his light and hues
Often, I ignore him, at times I give one or two courtesy smiles

He is envious
knowing I'm not his, still smiles and stares!
Unmoved by his wooing
I wait for my real ideal moon to cross the skies.

My ideal moon crosses light year distances every midnight
And visits me above my terrace
He spreads warmth over me, with his moon light
He satiates my longing every night.

Our mating makes my eyes glow, my cheeks grow rosy
He too forgets the hardship of travelling distances, seeing
me in delight of his company

The other moon above, is a dream for many stars
They twinkle and try to seduce him,
Write love quotes on him, shine brighter to woo him lustrously!
The other moon naughty, ignores none, as he is flirtatious,
loves company of those twinkling stars

My moon too, is the desire of many damsel-stars
He knows this, but in response only gives a smile!
He knows that he rightly belongs to me,
and I know I have him as mine
Thousands of miles in distance couldn't wither our love,
It flourishes more, every midnight!

The other moon stationed above my terrace, envies my
ideal moon
As he knows, he is too pale and charmless in front of my
beloved moon!
He knows his charm is transient and lasts only a day or
two
Being a crescent, he becomes frustrated for not being able
to get anyone to woo!

But my love never lets my moon deform even for a day
He is always full moon in the blue sky
And keeps his glitter every day!

Sitting on the corner of the sky above, the moon smiles
now
Connecting us in his dream, lost in each other
We are cosy together inside a shawl I've woven, it has the
softness of my love's yarn.

My moon will never ever be gone.

❑

The Lonely Church

Once I was lost in the dense wood on a snowy winter,
I kept wandering to find a shelter.

Hungry and thirsty I was with least little fervour
I prayed to God to become my Saviour

Then I sighted a donjon in a distance
Seeing it, my happiness knew no bounds

It was a white castle, isolated and lonely
With a sturdy red painted door standing profoundly

A lake nearby mirrored its image
As if it was a gallant wounded soldier resisting enemies
with utmost prowess!

The castle seemed quite old
As if for a long time it was left abandoned

Hunger or curiosity- I'm unsure what made me come closer
With little effort I could open the door and enter

But inside the castle…a bolt from the blue… waited a
surprise new
As I saw it was not an old castle but a Church without a hue.

A few spiders were busy making their webs
And some rats were playing hide and seek among
themselves.

The Altar was empty, the Church was barren,
Neither the Holy Mother, nor I, could find the Holy Son!

Suddenly I heard a queer sound coming from the Altar
I felt the Holy Mother was sobbing and uttering in
despair!

"This place is no more meant for us
So long there remains bloodshed, theft, hatred and fights
amongst brothers!

Violence and malice always keep men away and bereft of
our blessings
And all the holy places will remain alone and abandoned
with empty altars kept within!"

Hunger

Who am I?
What's my name?
I don't know
Someone calls, " Hey you!
Dirty girl!"
Some others say, "Gosh!
She's a shit!"
Who am I?
What's my name?
I don't know.

Near the temple,
Stands an old Banyan tree
Here down is lying a
Broken dustbin for long
This bin is my home !
I sleep there, eat
Whatever I find in that bin!
The insane old woman says,
I was found there!
In that bin!
In the darkness of the night
Someone came, threw me in that bin
and stealthily went back
To keep intact the whiteness of
All they clad!

But somehow, I could survive
And in the daylight
Same this 'I' became
A 'shit' or a 'filth'
For the society, for the humanity!
Is it so?
What nonsense that old woman says!

Everything else is fine with me
Only the problem is
I get hungry too often!
I remain unfed
For a whole day or two even!
Lots of mouldy food are thrown
In that broken dustbin throughout the day
But no one allows me to go
Near that bin
And fetch food.

Why shouldn't I go there ?
It's my home after all!
I've full right to go there!
Since birth I've been living there!
That broken bin is
My sweet home
My only shelter!
But no one understands that.
Earlier, the old priest of the temple
Used to give me something to eat.
Out of love or compassion
I don't know!
And I used to efface my hunger
At least for one time in a day!

But of late a young priest has
Taken over the charge of the temple.
He has vowed to clean up
The filth and impurity of the society.
So nowadays, I don't get anything to eat
From that dustbin.

This hunger is so strange!
It means something for someone
And something else for someone else!
If I don't get anything to eat
For a day or two even
I can satiate my hunger
Drinking water only.
But what about
The hunger of the body?
The hunger for flesh?
That drags people to the dustbin
In the darkness of the night!
They are bound to come
Closer to this stinky bin
Every now and then
To throw out their indigestion
To throw out the leftover!
And thus, letting another 'filth' similar to me
To pop up from the bin!
How strange!
People say, I'm a shit!
People say, I'm impure!
I'm a curse upon society!
I'm illegitimate!
Am I really illegitimate?
No!

Illegitimate is that hunger.
After satisfying which
People are bound to come near
To this stinky bin in the night
To throw all that they couldn't digest
While passing by it
They become reluctant in the daylight!

Who am I?
I don't know!
But I'm not illegitimate for sure.
Illegitimate is... that hunger.

❑

Journey

Walking through the myriad of thorns,
Scattered on the path of life,
Holding each other's thoughts together,
Glued with a pied floret-
Our maiden hope,
Life hasn't been so beautiful
If you weren't there,
To cling us firmly
Becoming our root!

The Stories

Deep inside all stories, there lives a secondary story About
something that is untold
About something that is unheard
Sometimes they lose words to be well expressed
Sometimes they become dumb, their lips being mercilessly
stitched!

While facing the struggle of spoken and unspoken feelings
inside
Some stories even deny their existence
Dream and reality -
In two convenient parts they share their lives easily
In the weighing scale of reality, these stories pull down
their desires easily!

Some inner stories are shredded into pieces
To keep them incomplete for life
Still they silently keep on trying to glean
The broken parts of their 'shredded selves'
And stringing them together carefully
Reveal themselves withstanding the repression.

The woman is one such beautiful story, though
incomplete…!

The Birds' Story

A pair of cute birds was sitting on my window pane
The female bird was blue eyed - as white as ivory
Her male counterpart was a little spotty.
She had many admirers she knew…
But her love for him was pure and true.
She was young, soft and passionate.
He loved her most, yet seemed to suspect her of late
They're busy with their tacit emotions:
One seemed to be weeping in silence,
The other sulking because of his inner darkness.

I was a silent on looker
Watching her irresistible beauty and his veiled scare
Suddenly he left with no direction
Leaving her swamped in blood of uncut wound
Distrust and disrespect perhaps led the relationship to get crumbled
And I was left dumb and grief stricken
As if the cute birds were a human couple !

An Unwritten Verse of Forbidden Love

Dear O' Dear!
When I die, don't hurry to my grave
Just throw from a distance
A handful of soil to the mud blanket
 Made for me to lie in eternal existence!
I don't want your favourite shirt to be stained in muddy
spots
While others stitch a soiled gown to cover my mortal
remains.
Rather I yearn to feel your solo presence on a vibrant
twilight
With your face reflecting a magical smile
To my forgotten soul, rays of light that presence would
shed
Helping me smile even beneath my destined eternal bed !
Being with you on such a night is the feeling of fresh
Jasmine and roses added to my tomb
To keep me loved throughout my eternal existence.
Be that solo Knight, my love, to add fragrance to my night !

Use a small knife to pierce my soil gown
Engrave your magical verses of love with it that you
wanted to write for me,
To make me feel cosy and your own!
Don't forget to inscribe the first letter of your name on my
gravestone after mine

I would feel happy so that even during afterlife it carries
your name with mine,
I cannot take it now when alive
At least let death bear yours as my surname and make the
world believe
I was yours forever,
And beyond that if ever!

My plight reminds me of 'Candida Morell - my favourite
female character
A woman so pure and feminine
Candida was the wife of a clergyman, in the 1904
theatrical performance
In the end, she had to choose between her husband and
her dream man
She had supported the weaker of the two, knowing it was
none other than her husband!
And that's how Candida ended staying with James, her
husband
Refusing Marchbanks, the one who had made her life
worthy to depend on!

But unlike Candida, I am not one so strong, but the one
feeble
Tamed and with both in me, conflicting in an emotional
battle!
I don't dare to choose him or you as one blind
Rather I'd choose death as my last bliss, and escape this
emotional fuss!
With you in real life, I couldn't add wings to our dream of
living together
Or peacefully hear your verse of love, written only for me,
Sometimes opening my eyes wide in wonder!

I can't be that 'Snow White, who you named me as once
I remember still, you whispering, "You're my Snow White,
a soul so pure and soft!"
that makes me forget every pain my life had given me!
You always had added bliss to my existence
Though being a poet, so insane and persistent!
Your verses are such that bear attraction
And reading it keeps all in connection!
But remember, the moment you pen it for me,
Just me, it never gets its affection, as our love is forbidden!
I'm living only as yours, but to others, the reality differs,
They see me as what I'm not, and this remains one big
ordeal!
It will only be seen as another verse of forbidden love
And will never get its due recognition as the one magical!
But do think, if I had died with the verse of love written
over my tomb
It will enlighten and embolden my soul to make the
eternal sleep content and whole!

O'Death!
Kiss me once and let me be what I want to be!
Can you?
My death would make my 'man' to the world a poetic
mentor
Keeping him the shining star to new verses as one
inventor!
And I would be known as that queen
Who inspired a poet to be known in the world as a literary
king!

An Ideal Wife

Today is India's traditional family faith
We call it 'Karva Chauth',
A mass prayer by the wives
For their husbands' welfare and health.

I have to keep a fast in his name
From sunrise to moonrise
Praying for his happiness,
Prosperity and health to appease.

To perform all the rituals in the evening,
I have to wear jewellery and the wedding dress
To be again a new bride
For him to exhibit me as his precious 'gain', his 'pride!

But the previous night, I was scratched,
Hit and bitten by his violent lust
And its marks seen all over my neck,
Hiding it from others today was a must.

I had to hide the scars on my face
from my neighbours, my sisters in law
To protect my family honour
From any human or laws.

So I didn't wait for the evening to paint my face
At dawn itself, against the rituals,
I stuffed concealers, powders and eyeliners
To hide my harassed trace!

That's my story as a wife
Who was born to be bitten with sharp fangs as a knife!

Today is the 'Karva Chauth'
During the rituals I have to bow down before my religious
faith
And beg for him long life, fortune and good health
Or in installments insults, scorns and assaults
To live on as an ideal wife!

❑

Being Alone

I was the youngest,
My siblings being older,
Prioritised last, and lone,
None to talk, none to play!

In the bouts of loneliness
I befriended my self
Talking to my 'inner self'!
I gave her a gender, named her 'she'!
Yes, she was indeed a true friend
Unbiased, honest, yet imaginary!

Our bond grew,
Diminishing my loneliness,
She came often stealthily,
At times heartily, to giggle and play,
Hopscotch, mimicry, storytelling, singing
Dancing, painting, role playing
And beyond!
For me, a new world she built!
Like the Romans, she also seemed a Genie from the lamp!

One day, she spoke to me sad,
I was thirteen, and felt on that day very bad,
Her eyes were swollen, it's nerves all red,
But I read in it, a story with a sad ending

And felt she was here to put a full stop in our bonding
She hugged me hard with tears,
And whispered in my tiny ears,
"Let us part! Let me go!
You're grown and strong,
Pampering you more is wrong!
I will rest hereafter inside your heart,
I know, it's your most sensitive part
Touch your heart when you miss me,
That's where I will stay forever...!"

Saying this, she vanished from my sight
And left a vacuum in thought,
I felt heartbroken and dumb,
I felt my legs were rooted to earth
With some hardened glue, making me immobile!

Days, weeks, months and years passed
Now a mother of my son,
At his age of three, I am his best friend,
His playmate, his Santa!
He doesn't need an imaginary friend
Coz, I was there to complete him!
But I remain at times lonely,
I still miss my inner self, my only companion!
I softly press my heart to feel her
And ask myself,
"Am I still alone?"

❏

When I Hold My Golden Pen
(Dedicated to my loving father)

When I was only nine
My dad gifted me a golden pen.
With some blue ink
He himself did it fill,
And asked me to write
A word of my choice.
Without thinking much
I wrote a word on a paper,
My name it was!

But the pen was new to me
And with its sharp nib
I could write my name hardly legible to him!
He asked me to write it again,
And I kept on writing my name
On that piece of paper until I saw it's shining!
A smile came to me automatically
And dad too smiled and left the room silently.

Since then, that golden pen
Became my constant companion!
My last resort, my only solace!
And when I'm about to fall
While facing life's ordeals,
I tightly hold my golden pen

And feel as if it bequeaths me
All its might and whispers,
"My dear!
Hold me tight!
And don't get scared of life.
Grip me firmly
And write, write! "

On each blank paper it scribbles my tears!
Sometimes lets my tears melt,
Sometimes lets them dry,
Sometimes it elaborates my happiness with ink roseate!
Many times, it describes my thoughts
Many times, it fills my mood
Assembling all the colours I like!

Throughout my life, I couldn't make my dad proud
Couldn't rise up to his hopes.
But I was and I am always his pupil of eyes!
And to see me at the heights
He did all without compromise!
How wisely my dad knew it,
That all the time he won't be able to stand by me!
Sometimes time, sometimes distance, sometimes other issues
Won't let him stay with me.
So, he gifted me that golden pen
To be with me, to support me,
To stand by me in sunshine and rain,
To wipe out my tears, to lessen my pain!

When I hold my golden pen
I remember my dad's wish

To see my name shining
Through my poems I write
With my golden pen!

When I hold my golden pen
I feel my dad's patting on my back,
I feel my dad's sitting beside me,
Though he is living in his divine residence, far away from
me ...!

Love Berg

She was always frozen as ice
Not knowing what's in her eyes!
The moment his sight gently touched her shivering lips
The glacier built for years in her heart
Split, and was no longer a part of
All the long felt frozen pain
In her heart drifted now as a gain!
Even the vacuum felt in her eyes
Floated around as powdered ice
Moving into a sea of heaven
Where love united from uneven
It showed her better light
Adding wings to her flight!
Love which was once frozen
Is now floating like icebergs
In the sea of haven ...!

Solace

In the lonely road of life
In deep darkness
When I lost the way,
I was robbed
Of all my belongings
My emotions, my feelings!
I wanted to shout,
I wanted to scream,
I wanted to cry aloud,
But I didn't!
Because something precious
Was still there with me,
And that was you
With your absence!
And I realized,
I hadn't lost myself
Ah! What a solace!

A New Relationship

Here we are
After a long decade unaware!
Should I ask
How are you, dear?
Do you still feel near?
Or expect you to ask me the same
Sooner or later?
For some time, can we hear each other?
Or remain silent for another hour?
What will you desire or prefer?

Listen!
Happiness we have shared in lots
Joy we had in places and varied spots!
Now let's share some sorrow without fear
Some confessional moments and tears!
Let's share some deepfelt loneliness
Some life failures with a true willingness!

Let the tears roll down our cheeks, freely
Don't try stopping them cruelly
Like a freshet, let them flow
To remove pain of the wounded hearts
So that the grief never again keeps us apart!
After the fallout
Let the broken breaths do a callout!

On each other without any more pain
Let's add in it, a few drops of joy like the first rain!

Let's sow some fresh seeds
of a new hope without any more weeds
Let's think something new
Let's live a relation, crystal clear as dew
Let it be from today
Let's weave a new story, let's smile everyday
You want it to remain unnamed?
If so I have no other choice but to bear the same life
untamed.

Love of a Kind

I don't know how to peep inside his heart
A shield of human anatomy doesn't allow me that part!

When I look straight into his eyes
I see a reflection on the rise!

This reflection resembles myself,
And smiles at me unknowingly from himself!

People say the richest feeling is love!
A heavenly feel on earth, a treasured affection cove!

But the feeling, which wraps us together,
Is something beyond and richer!

It has comfort, solace, adds charm to our souls
It speaks of many attitudinal tools!

The precious smile bejewelled on our lips
Togetherness gives us life's many tips!

What else do we need then?
Commitment, promises
That we wouldn't move apart!
No! Certainly not !

We talk
We share
We care...
Unconditionally...!

Can it be called love?
Perhaps not
Definition spoils the thrill.

Set it free
Let it be unnamed,
He and me,
The something undefined!

The Burden

A little foetus was sobbing inside its mother's womb
As that day was its last day with its beloved mom!
As in the next morning, it's right to see this beautiful
world would be taken away!
A girl child's foetus it was: the only reason of this brutal
slay!

In that morning, the little foetus heard its mom pleading
to her 'man'
Not to kill it brutally, not to barren her womb!
But the man was determined to shed the burden
Not a daughter but a son he needed
To secure his old age, to ensure a place for him in Heaven!

In the evening, the mom lighted an earthen lamp in front
of the idol of her deity
She was silent, but her eyes were vocal and teary!
Like the faint ray of light that the little earthen lamp was
carrying with
The mom had also been keeping alive
a faint hope inside her:
That a miracle would happen!
And she won't be bereft of this Bliss of Heaven!
But she didn't know that like her and the little foetus,
Helpless was the deity too!

The ill-starred night was about to end
The jolly dawn was ready to welcome the first day of
'Navaratri'
'Navaratri' - the glorification of 'Adi-Shakti', the divine
feminine creative power
The celebration of the victory of good over evil, deception
and treachery!
For nine days, a pot was to be installed in a hallowed place
With a lamp to be kept lit on the pot
But before that, it was the time to abort the foetus!
It was, indeed, the time to forsake the 'burden' ...!

❑

Wonder Morning

Kiss my eyelids each morning
Awakening my reality by transforming my dreams and
yearning!

Lock my lips each morning
Squeezing out all the vacuum that remained in me, darling!

Quench my thirst each morning
that remained unsatiated for long
Pouring your virility deep within me to drench!

Hug me tight each morning
Spreading your warmth around me as a warm blanket
vague!

Explore me each morning
Making it a bliss, the one kind that reminds me of heaven
to implore...

❑

The Wiser Woman

Was it the curse on Eve who had once eaten a fruit
forbidden?
Jealousy and insecurity are still considered as attributes
that glorify a woman!

When someone achieves, what makes a woman so jealous?
They act weird, when the other person is from a similar
genus!

What prevents two women from appreciating each other's
acumen?
Understand that efforts are applied for survival by all women!

The clamour usually begins with,
"OMG! She's become more popular, more successful than
me!"
"Oops! She added more fan-followers on Insta, Facebook
or Twitter than me!"
"She looks prettier, her dark circles void and crow's feet
all gone!
Is it because she's happier than me, or is it because of the
special effects from the camera of her latest phone?"

The moment such thoughts pollute a female mind
She leaves even a delicious dish half cooked on the gas
stove, and rushes to find a destroying solution fine!

Anxiety makes her lose appetite or a deep sleep
Sometimes even ends up taking anti depression pills, to
get a slumber deep!

My dear pretty Eves! Rise up wise, don't step into that
stone age trap again!
Don't be enticed by that fruit which was long declared
forbidden!

Instead, allow your hearts to plant some seeds of love,
compassion and positivity
Their growing buds can only kill the satanic germs of
jealousy, envy, hatred and insecurity!

You may be a writer, an actor, an academician or a
business woman.
But know it well, thou can excel in your field only with
skills, hard work and basic intelligence!

It's time to restrict the rounds of cancerous Satans!
Support your fellow beings, by being their angel guardians!

O' pretty dames! Let today's Shakespeares edit their
scripts about you
Let them erase that word 'frailty that often describes you!

When it comes to all women, ask them to write strength
and let the world know
Though soft hearted, Eves have become stronger and
smarter now!

The Last Letter

O' my dear!
My beautiful wife!
For you, this is my last letter
Written not in a scented paper
But in a torn piece
With my fresh blood all splattered!

I was laughing at a joke, one dear to me
But that joke is now a corpse fallen near to me!
I am shot and soon will become another to follow the trial!
Who's there here, to call a corpse by his name!
It's just a number soon,
With no name of my own?

I am a soldier and am proud to be!
But my dear, I could not leave anything for my posterity!
I am proud of having you,
My beautiful wife!
Without me now onwards,
Your beauty will put you in strife!
People call us their saviours!
Like Hawks, we perpetually hook our eyes around,
On the enemies and those intruders who come to gamble!
We control and guard our nation's border
To save its honour from all such perilous invaders!
For us, days and nights mean the same

Sacrificing our leisure to the assigned duties we perform
Today people sleep peacefully and live happier
But unsafe are our homes in our absence
And even when we are alive and present
But alas, in the border!

❑

The Recipe of Love

A handful of anger,
Few pinches of resentment,
A couple of drops in tears,
Sometimes continue over the years!
All blended together,
With a sprinkle of smile
Like salt to a dish!
An ideal pray to live on
At one's own wish!

Taste it, o' dear!
It's neither so sweet nor sour,
But does in similar angles pour!
You may find it quite queer,
But more or less it's the same for every peer!
For me, what's so dear
Is love around, keeping it near!
The perfect recipe made ever,
The one which glorifies forever!

Problem is Never the End

When you feel quite low
Situations may demand you to bow
Try turning over the page and giving a look
At your son's sketch book!

You will discover his dad drawn as his hero,
You would have never been drawn in that as a zero,
He would have glorified all your avatars with a great intro

When you're frustrated,
Amidst problems deep rooted
Look stealthily into your wife's eyes
She neither complains or cries,

When she sees your presence, she may look simple,
But her eyes will always be bright with a twinkle

When you come home stressed or sad,
Or haunted by problems that turn you mad,
Check where's your mom, that evening,
You will find her, in front of her religious faith praying
Not for herself, but your good health, prosperity and well
being!

One commits suicide without thinking and dies
But due to his untimely demise
Does it make his siblings or loved ones wise?

Never they will be at ease
Rather they will suffer more, and never rise
Your death kills them thousand times more,
Making their life hell and sore

Killing yourself in depression
Gives only more pain and suppression

Does it provide a solution?
Never my friend!
You are in an illusion
And the most wronged direction!
Take challenges of life and live smiling as a fixed
resolution
All problems in due time, gives also its ideal solution

Problems only make you bend,
But it's never your end!

Survived Bird

I was a hapless bird
Imprisoned in a golden cage!

I was pining to breathe fresh air
Under the open sky!

I was longing to break that invisible chain
My legs were all this while 'chained!

I slept reminiscing those days,
When I used to chirp and hop,
Singing the song of hope.

You have given me now courage
To break this rusted chain,
Which had wounded my hopes and brain.

Now I started to value,
The strength in my wings

I am ready to surge upward,
And getting prepared to fly.

Be that uplifting wind,
Under my strong wings,

Be for me that widened sky,
Watch me soaring greater heights!

O' Jesus! Please be Reborn!

He was a carpenter
Later one ideal teacher
A preacher, a saviour
A true Christian he was
The Holy Son
He was our Jesus!
They killed him in three hours of a whim:
Dragged and, brutally tortured Him
He was hung by his hands and nailed to a horizontal beam
wooden
Enormous torture a human could hardly bear
He bore it all without pain or fear!
What was the Holy Son's Sin?
Neither a thief He was,
Nor a killer or adulterer He was!
But He was sentenced to death!
Caesar's trustworthy Pilate
Was the one behind such a devilish plan.
For them, He was a sinner!
Because He wanted to spread the message of God and
make public a winner!
He wanted to raise man from their drunken stupor, and
restore peace
He wanted to teach the sweetest language
The one of compassion and love
His soul was pure as one snow white dove!
He wanted to pull up the good
Burying evil for good!

The only Sin He could do,
Was not to protest or ask for mercy
Till His last breath, people only heard him saying,
"Father, forgive them!
For they don't know what they're doing!"
Rising up into the sky
He left for His heavenly abode
Keeping a hope alive in His mind
That sooner or later His sacrifice
Will make the lives worth living
for mankind!
With every passing century
His eyes shed pearly tears in utmost pain
For even now He feels cheated, his heart deeply bruised
As He saw His sacrifice went in vain
For whom He put His life at stake
Humans still are oblivious of their mistakes.
Oh Jesus! the Holy Spirit!
I am neither a Jew nor a Christian!
I read about you the way
I read about Cinderella or Hatim Tai!
But still I wish, Oh Jesus! Please be reborn!
Please come to earth and live amidst us!
O' Holy Father! please send again
Your favourite Son to this chaotic earth!
Not to sacrifice His life once again
But to save mankind
To teach us how to learn
The art of worthy living.
Please be reborn our Saviour
We will treat you warm and with fervour!

❑

An Ode to Freedom

O' dear!
The song I could never sing
The dream I could never dream
Without you!

O' dear!
Without you, I was a bird with two wings
But could never learn how to fly!
Without you, I was a honey bee
But never knew how to buzz!

Now I'm a lark, who's singing the song of life!
Now I'm a dreamer, dreaming of a better world full of
hope!
I'm a poet, letting my ink dive deep into the ocean of
imagination with ease!
I'm a woman, surpassing all the hurdles of life
Who's now ready for a journey towards the east without a
cease!
Now people ask me your identity with curiosity!
In reply, I give them a smile of sublimity!
How can I tell them who you're to me?
O' dear!
My sense of freedom!
You're who I've recently found sprouted inside me!
You've freed me from the shackles of my self-made
inadequacy!

❏

A Storm and a Maiden Dream

A maiden dream and a handful of hopes
She sows in her small garden
With utmost care she waters daily
The maiden dream and a handful of hopes
The dream gets sprouted
And rooted deeply the hopes that firmly cling to the dream.

She and he live in a thatched hut
When it rains, water drips from the roof
She counts the stars through the holes of the broken roof
And falling in his passionate embrace, sings the song of
life and love
Through the holes, the young new moon peeps and listens
And smiling he returns to his beloved moonshine.

But an unruly storm of *Phagun* has cruelly shattered all
Her thatched hut and the broken roof
Her maiden dream and a handful of sprouted hopes.
He will no longer return from the market with her
favourite fruit
The planted bomb has destroyed him from the root
The news has made her womb to bleed
As without him there's no life to lead!

Today again, she has started sowing and watering
No dream but only a handful of hopes

That one day this world will be free
From all storms and bombs
And no one will be bereft of a maiden dream,
Love and a handful of hopes.

The Phagun or the Phalgun is the eleventh month of the Hindu calendar, known for devastating storms.

❏

I Don't Want to be Desdemona

I wanted to fall in love with you!
But see! I couldn't!
Certainly, I was moved by your candid confession
And thought for a second,
Should I lessen my aloofness towards you?
Should I hear your voice of love,
And soften my heart for you?
But see! I couldn't!

I adjured you once,
"Please touch my heart, dear!"
You laughed and said,
"You're like a Jasmine, flowering at night!
So beautiful you're!
Please let me come into your life like Othello!
And you will be my Desdemona!
Forever, for sure!"

"No, no!
I don't want to be another Desdemona!
Neither a Kamala Das nor another Silvia Plath!
As I'm replete with an honest affection, true and deep!
Look there! They're waiting!
My daughter and the umbra of my being!
Your obsession is simply a deception, I'm sure
I don't want to be a Desdemona anymore!"

❏

The Girl Who has Refused to be Born!

A woman was screaming in utmost labour pain
As she was on the threshold of motherhood pristine!
Everyone in the family was happy to imagine
The arrival of a little doll!
But even after a period of long 15 hours,
The doctors couldn't make her deliver the child
Why? Why? Why?
With every passing moment, the question
Spun round rapidly in everyone's mind!
Like the leaves whirled in eddies of wind...!

In Heaven, a 'girl' foetus was sobbing!
God, the Creator, came to her, and asked her lovingly
"Dear! Why are you sobbing?
Why are you still here?
For your pleasant arrival your beloved mom
And the family both are desperately waiting!
Go! Go back to your mom's womb!
For you, with open arms, a beautiful world outside is
eagerly waiting!"
The girl foetus stopped sobbing
And replied vehemently,
"No! No!
I don't want to be born!
Though I know, for me my mom and dad,
Both are desperately waiting!

When I was in mom's womb
I could hear their conversation!
Mom-dad wanted the baby to be a girl!
They were preparing to welcome a 'Laxmi'!
What not they were dreaming about me!
My education, my upbringing, my marriage even!!
Dreaming the dream, they kept on laughing!
And in the tears that're oozing from their eyes in ecstasy
Their happiness started diving!
I too was happy to be born as their daughter beloved!
To love them from the core of my heart and thus get
loved!
But, oh Father! I have changed my mind now
I am not going to be born in that world created by you
The then beautiful world is now not safe for us girls
Instead of 'men', there live 'vampires' and 'cannibals'!
They eat the raw fleshes of innocent girls!
They love to suck and drink their fresh blood!
They don't even hesitate to play with
The private parts of a 'female' body, of a two- or five-year-
old!
Like dolls, they play with the bodies of those innocent
girls, who're yet to grow up!
Those body parts, which were still tiny and yet to
develop!"
"No! Father!
I am not going to be born!
As I am afraid, my mom would be able to
Save me from being torn!"
God stood still, He remained dumb!
He had no option but to support her decision, with an
upright thumb!

The doctors finally decided to go for an urgent C - Section
As they have tried and failed with all possible options!
Everyone in and outside the Operation Theatre was
Praying for a safe delivery
Pleading God to let the moment come a little early
After an hour, the much-awaited moment came!
And leaving all heartbroken and dumbstruck
The doctors found the sac empty, filled with amniotic
fluids only...!

❑

Love Again

O' my dear!
O' my man!
I kept on falling in love with you,
But I didn't realize
You came to me like a rover to an inn!

Again, and again, I trusted you
Again, and again, you cheated me!
Again, and again, you went away from me
Unfurling my dreams and my desires with glee!

Again, and again in dawn or twilight
Again, and again in sunshine or rain
With eyes teary and a heart redden
I sat like a moot with a question to put
Why is it so tough to forget someone?
And my heart smiled and replied,
"There's one feeling pristine resides within you
That tempts you to fall in love
With the same man again and again
You loved him then, you still love him
And you will keep on falling in love
Always with the same man!
Again, and again!
Again, and again...!"

❏

Imagination

Often, I imagine a land of beauty
To sit calm, quiet and write my poetry
In a city of concrete where I dwell
I can only imagine nature in its bounty.

When I look around, I find
Everyone is so busy!
They're so habituated to their everyday life:
Their boring and robotic life!

My imagination and me
We've a beautiful bonding
It often takes me to a land of fairies, to my village,
To relive my childhood days!
It tempts me to write, it forces me to live!

Here I'm!
I'm bound to live in this city
Shouldering my duties and amidst my people
O' God!
Please don't deprive me of my only relief
O' God!
Please let my imagination be forever with me.

She and a Cup of Cappuccino

Here we are,
In the same old coffee shop
We used to come and sit together,
Perhaps, for the last time!
Taking the last sip
From a cup of cappuccino
With two cubes of sugar.

Until today, my heart was her sole refuge!
A poor lover I am
Who couldn't give her riches, huge
Tomorrow, she will not be mine
She has to forget this poor guy
And accept another man's surname to sign!

Earlier I preferred espresso with no sugar
As my life was the same:
It's taste was only bitter!
She came and I started liking
Cups of cappuccino, sweet and foamy.
In her company, I became a changed man
Ever happy and not at all gloomy!

Now it's time for us to depart
I've to wish her a new life and then we'll part
I smile at her though my heart is heavy
From day after tomorrow, I've to learn a lot of things:
To live without her and my favourite cup of coffee.

❏

A Few Words of False Hope

Every morning in my eyes
I wear a beautiful smile,
And the fragrance of
That Jasmine smile
Tempts a pair of pale eyes
To glitter for a while!

After each sleepless night
In the morning I plead with my eyes,
Not to let the tears flow!
As seeing my smiling eyes
A new day begins,
A wish and a hope grow!

I cram,
A few words of hope daily!
Though false,
They work miraculously!
As the resonance of
Those words of hope
Compels a tired heart
To beat unceasingly!
Those words of false hope
Reverberate like holy chants,
For a cause divine!
They've been spoken persistently

To tempt someone to live
Not for a while, but continually!

Of late, I've been charged of
Being a deceiver, a liar and a sinner!
People bully me, throw stones
Of sharp words at me!
But I've neither to react nor to retort,
As they don't know
I've left no stones unturned!
And a bunch of those fictitious words
Is now for me the last resort
The only shaft to cling, the only pillar to hold up!

Nowadays I don't know
What's a lie or what's the truth!
What's a deceit or what's a sin!
Trust me, I don't know
As I've vowed to keep on telling lies
To pour a few drops of life in a dying soul...

❏

Smile

A smile is enough to hide the pain kept
Within you for so long
And make people happy while
Listening to your saddest song!

A smile is enough to make the world
Envious of your happiness
Though it is at the cost of a
Tainted soul's fruitful business!

A smile is enough to cover the scars
Of your bruised heart
And let the world know
You are a painter, an expert!

A smile is needed in
Life's every stage
A smile is none but
A 'life in camouflage!

The Mask

O' woman!
How helpless you are!
Very often you need to hide the beauty of your face
With a facade or a mask!
Is it a compulsion or in the name of protection?
Is it for protecting your delicate skin from direct sunlight?
Or to guard yourself from some lecherous eyes?

O' woman!
How helpless you are!
How often you need to hide your beautiful face with a
mask!
Have you seen faces wearing masks like you ?
Not to protect… not to guard !
They keep on wearing masks
To hide their ugliness from us!
When those masks get unveiled one after another…
You can see how selfish and vicious their faces appear!

O' woman!
Though many a times you remain behind a mask!
The beauty of your face and your soul
Will remain unflawed and untouched!

❏

Symbiosis

In her lonely moments
Amidst a crowd
When her heart was sobbing
In utter pain and despair
A sudden thought came and crept
Into her heart stealthily
Making her feel his presence beside her
Even in his absence
A smile bloomed on her face unknowingly!

Unspoken

Sometimes the heart bleeds!
It screams with utmost pain
Of un-shown wounds
At the loss of trust!
Like a flashy fountain, tears flow
To wipe out the frozen stains of blood!
Many a time they succeed
To reduce those stains
And the heart gets a little relief.

Tears!
How mighty they're!
But are they able to remove the scars beneath?
Perhaps not!
As very often those scars glitter
As in them, past memories infuse life
And they remain unconcealed…!
They remain uncured…!

The Gardener

She got sprouted,
In the garden of his heart.
He watered her daily,
Nurtured her to bloom.
He touched her cosily,
And vowed to keep her
Away from gloom.
His cosy touch made her
Blush every time,
Those unspoken words of
Love between them
Together formed a feminine rhyme!

With his gentle caress
She soon turned out
To be a pied floret!
So beautiful, so wispy,
So soft, so delicate!
Her elegance, her beauty
Fascinated everyone
Her sweet-smelling fragrance
Imbued all around!

Her alluring beauty
Made him worried,
What if someone comes and

Brutally plucks her out!
So, to save her irresistible beauty
From the lustrous eyes
Of every passer-by,
He decided to cling her firmly
Becoming her root!

The Travelogue of Love

She wanted to dive deep into his eyes
And find the source of that innocent look
That had silently knotted her with him
For once, only for once!
She wanted to enter his heart stealthily
And touch his heartbeats with her lips
For once, only for once!
She wanted to introduce her fingers with that touch
And feel the tingling of his heart
For once, only for once!
She walked up to his heart tip-toed
To break his pride, to salve his wounds
With her maiden touch!
But she never knew he was boastful
About that untouched corner of his heart,
And the myriad wounds
Which were hidden in that corner!
Somehow, he could sense her presence
At the threshold of his heart!
And without a mercy he teared off
The travelogue from her to him,
She wrote with the ink of her solemn love...!

An Ode to You, O' My Dear!

O' my dear!
When I recall you,
I feel the fragrance of your soul!
I feel as if I'm in a prayer hall
Hearing the holy chants
And reading the gospel!
Your presence in my life is so pristine
As the ringing of the Church bell!

Do you remember the dream I shared with you?
That on the bank of Yamuna, I was waiting for you!
That night was full moon
And with every moment passing by
I was desperate and behaving like a loon!
I was so lustrous to fall in your embrace
To merge with you, to feel you at my best!
But suddenly I heard your enchanting voice
You're calling me by my name of your choice!
Suddenly your voice turned out to be
The melody of the Divine Flute!
And in no time, I became 'Meera Bai'*!
Without knowing it's real or moot!

❏

(Meera Bai was a Hindu saint, a mystic poet and a devotee of Lord Krishna)

So What if You're a Daughter?

So what if you're a daughter?
A 'son' or a 'daughter' is
Mere a word that defines a gender!
Being a daughter doesn't determine
The inner capabilities or strength of a particular kind,
That you're feeble, tamed or both combined!
What actually matters is how perfectly you shoulder
The responsibilities towards your parents,
Especially towards your mother,
In absence of her loving husband and your doting father!

Trust me!
It doesn't matter that you're a daughter!
Raise your dampened soul and wipe your floating eyes!
Be liberal, be patient and fill her life
With all positive vibes!
Be brave, be bold, be wise
And show the world how strong you're!
Fight courageously and protect your mother
From the odds and the evil eyes!

A Rhyme of Love

In the midst of a dreadful dream
As I was trembling all alone and sobbing
You came and held me tight
And asked me to close my eyes
As I did,
My fear disappeared.

As I was trying to write something,
But unable to do so, I was only scribbling,
You came,
With a gift for me.
It was a bottle of roseate ink!
I filled my pen with it and composed the most beautiful
script
That I had ever written in my life,
A rhyme of love, that was!

The Fear

I'm getting old
The wrinkles on my face
Are clearly visible now!
I am afraid
Lest along with my waning age
May your memories not be blurred!

❑

Determination

Listening to her Dad's bedtime stories
Like a spider, she knitted a world of her own With tales
and fairies!
In the stories, her little mind found free expression
And she grew up with two invisible wings of imagination!
Dad told her the story of Robert Bruce
Defeated and fallen as he was, Hopes he was bound to
lose!
But a little spider showed him the way to rise
He got up and vowed to touch again the highs!
When she grew up, she read Satan
In Paradise Lost and Paradise Regained
The spirit of Milton's Satan allured her much
And she learnt how to reawaken the 'self' From a fallen
state as such!

A woman she's now - deep and fully grown
She's realized, life's a battlefield
With enemies known and unknown!
But like Bruce, she's confident, having the Satan's will
Determined she is - not to fall at any moment
And not to leave her dreams unfulfilled.

Not in My Name

[*A tribute to the sixteen years old boy named Junaid, who was brutally killed in a train*]

An innocent soul
Was forced to leave
This beautiful world
Of the Holy Creator!
He was sobbing,
Tears trickled down his eyes
Like an unruly stream flowing.
He was only sixteen
Junaid was his earthly name!

The soul went to the Creator
And once asked:
"O' Father! Why me?
Why I wasn't allowed to live
In that beautiful world,
You've created?
What's my fault?
What's my sin?
Was I a terrorist?
A fraud?
An adulterer?
A sinner?
No!
I just grew up to adolescence;

As pure as a budding bloom
As innocent a soul
As naïve a young calf
Caressed by its mother!

My sin was that
I looked a little 'different'!
My crime
I wore a skull cap!
And more than that
Beard had started
Sprouting on my chin!

Such a big crime!
Unpardonable!
I looked different!
They went on beating me;
I was crying, pleading, shouting
Leave me!
Please!
For Heaven's sake!
But I wasn't heard!

Who're they?
I don't know.
What's their religion?
I never guess.
What's their colour?
I never noticed.
What do they wear?
I never bother.
I remember mine
I was wearing green

A colour of nature and harmony
Freshness and energy.
Who're they again?
I may guess:
They're anonymous
Loveless and angry 'mob'
Who learn only to hate
In the name of religion!

I was so happy
Knowing that
A celebration was at hand!
A celebration after
A long trail of tough living!
A celebration of love and brotherhood
A celebration after a
Mass prayer for humanity!
But I couldn't be a part of it!

O' Father!
It is for sure:
You haven't taught anyone
To hate, to contempt
To fight or to look down upon!
But I doubt that you know:
Your Hymns of love
Have been misspelled for years
Your messages of humanity
Have been wrongly conveyed
To man on earth,
Your beautiful creation!
So much chaos, so much blood shed
So much misunderstanding

In your Garden of Eden prevailing
In the name of colour
In the name of religion
In the name of you,
The Creator even!
Wake up, o' Father!
Save the world mad
Save the mortals
From committing more sin
Restore trust and faith
So that no other Junaid
Would be killed!
No killing again; and
Not in My Name!
Bridge in love, patience
And endurance; but
No killing again; and
Not in My Name!

The Task

Sometimes
She digs her own grave,
Then sitting comfortably inside it
She carefully strings together
All the broken parts of her self
That she has gleaned.

❑

An Untold Love Story

No one knew who she was
A greenish beauty
Like the mermaid in the water
She would be the mermaid of the wood!

A young man of twenty
Once saw her in the wood
She was playing in the lake water
And he was peeping at her
From a leafy bower.
The sprinkling sunshine
Enhanced her heavenly charm
A Lark and a Mynah came flying and sat on her arm
Soon she disappeared from his sight
Spell bound as he was
Oblivious of if it was day or night!

Every day he visited the place
To have a glimpse of her
Only he got disappointed
As she didn't appear.

A couple of days later
Happiest he became, as he saw her again!
She was playing in the lake water
Singing a soothing song

The Lark and the Mynah too were
Accompanying her in the song.
Spreading his colorful feathers
A peacock too was nearby dancing.
The scene was so pleasant
That one can hardly describe in words
Mesmerized the young man was
By her bewildering beauty
He could not decide
If it was a truth or a fancy.
He was so stunned by
The beauty fluorescent
That soon he caught in a reverie
As if he was in the garden of Eden!

Suddenly she saw him peeping
Stealthily she came and caught him dreaming
So shocked he was that
Dumb stricken he remained!
He tried to speak
But murmured in vain!

She came closer
And smiled at him
She held his chin lightly
Kissed him for a while gently
With tears in her eyes
She stared at him for a few seconds
And vanished from his sight
Leaving there only her fragrance!

From that day onwards
No one saw the young man again

In his small cottage
A young maiden of his village
Found a painting of a pied beauty
With greenery all around her!

The painting is with an old lady today
Who's supposed to be that young maiden,
Who too loved him,
Though her love remained pent up
And hidden.

❑

Note of Appreciation

Poems from the quill of a very sensitive poet

Dr. Pabitrapran Goswami

Malakshmi Borthakur is my Facebook friend. I know her as a poet and a classical singer. I have got the first taste of her poetry in Facebook itself. *Splendid Signature: Rhythmic Strokes of a Quill* is supposed to be the first collection of her poems. I had the pleasure of going through the manuscript as she wanted me to do so with the request for an editorial support. After reading the poems, I could not stop myself from writing a few words for her.

Malakshmi is a very sensitive poet. Her language is simple, yet expressive and strong. Love seems to be a dominant theme of her poetry, besides other curses of civilisation, viz., poverty, hunger, child labour, insecurity of women etc. Malakshmi is very sensitive about gender equality and is in favour of women empowerment. She is also in love with nature and is capable of r105eading even the feelings and emotions of birds and animals.

I wish Malakshmi a bright and brilliant literary career and hope that *Splendid Signature: Rhythmic Strokes of a Quill* will get the proper appreciation of the readers.

❑

(Dr. Pabitrapran Goswami is an author, academician, musician and the former Principal of Jorhat College, Jorhat, Assam.)

Short Review

Book to own with pride

Sreekala P. Vijayan

When the symphony of soul and pen moves in rhythm, wonders are created. Malakshmi Borthakur's *Splendid Signature- Rhythmic Strokes of a Quill* is such a creation of a prolific pen, who loves nature and sings melodiously about her. Uniqueness of each poetic expression transforms this book into a must read for all ages. Multi angular view of the poet towards the socio-cultural issues provides the reader amusement and wisdom on the go.

Poems starting with uncertainty and ending with poetic ideologies bear the aesthetics of good poems. These attributes are very well seen throughout Malakshmi's creations. The world which she lives in has infinite uncertainties and unsolved issues. When tongue fails to aim the arrow precisely, the poet's ink does it. Unveiling of realities needs quite a good amount of mental strength. Malakshmi's prolific pen has showered the ink on such crucial issues. Her words are adorned with poetic wisdom and imagination, dragging the reader to the inner voices of the poet. Even the rustle of leaves, humming of bees turn on the writing moods of the poet.

A book becomes a success when it acts as a food for thought and further initiates the thinking capabilities of the readers. Captivating and content-oriented verses with a heuristic approach upholds the relatability to the reader, which holds one back to the chair to devour the fragrance of poetry while relaxing.

In a nutshell, the brilliant compilation of poems by the multilingual poet Malakshmi Borthakur is a *book to own with pride*. I wish *Splendid Signature-Rhythmic Strokes of a Quill* a successful global readership.

❑

(Sreekala P Vijayan is an internationally acclaimed award winning multi lingual poet and a best-selling author. She is the Academic In-charge for Soundarya Educational Trust, Bangalore, India)

Acknowledgement

Splendid Signature: Rhythmic Strokes of a Quill is a collection of 50 poems written in English. These multi- thematic poems are selected from a bulk of poems written during the period 2016 to 2021. The publication of a book of poems is a dream for a volatile person like me and the dream would never come true if some people were not in my life with their prayers, good wishes and blessings.

Words cannot express my gratitude to ...

K. Satchidanandan
Chairman, Kerala Sahitya Akademi, poet, translator, editor and academician
For writing the BLURB

Dr. Anand Prakash
Author, editor and former Professor of Delhi University.
For writing the INTRODUCTION

Dr. Pabitrapan Goswami
Author, academician, musician and the former Principal of Jorhat College, Assam.
For the EDITORIAL SUPPORT and writing a NOTE OF APPRECIATION

Sreekala P. Vijayan
Best-selling author and academician, Bangalore, India
For writing the BOOK REVIEW

Mr. Satya Pattanaik
Director, Black Eagle Books, USA
For the support in publishing the book

Mr. Ashok Parida
Bhubaneswar, Odisha, India
For COVER DESIGN & LAYOUT

My ever-supportive FAMILY:
the FOUR PILLARS of my life
Mrs. Dipali Borthakur - mother
Mrs. Nirmali Borthakur - sister
Dr. Biju Kumar Bhagawati - husband
Baby Ananya Madhubhashini - daughter.

The Sources of Inspiration and Well-Wishers

Mrs. Uma Rani Bezbora
Former English Teacher, Govt. Girls' H.S School, Jorhat, Assam.

Mr. Vijay Kumar Dewan
Senior Advocate, Guwahati High Court, Assam

Ms. Meera Mathur
Registrar, Bhatkhande Sangit Vidyapith, Lucknow, Uttar Pradesh

Pramod Kumar Jha
Former Director, Doordarshan - Ranchi, Jharkhand.

Mrs. Sunita Aron
Senior Resident Editor, Hindustan Times - Lucknow, Uttar Pradesh

Dr. Karabi Deka Hazarika
Eminent poet and author, Former Professor of Assamese, Dibrugarh University, Assam

Mr. Utpal Dutta
Author, critic and filmmaker, Guwahati, Assam

Dr. Jyotirekha Hazarika
Eminent poet and writer, Associate Professor - Assamese, J.B. College, Jorhat, Assam

Mr. Samir Baruah
Assistant Professor- English, Bahona College, Jorhat, Assam

Mr. Utpal Kalita
Associate Professor- English, LOKD College, Dhekiajuli, Sonitpur, Assam

Dr. Prakash Balikai
Assistant Professor – English, Central University of Karnataka, Karnataka

Mr. Kishore Baraskar
Founder of Parivartan'360, Life Coach and Motivational Trainer, Mumbai, Maharastra.

All My Friends And Readers

And above all
MY DAD IN HEAVEN
Late Sarat Chandra Borthakur

CONNECT TO THE POET

FACEBOOK
https://www.facebook.com/malakshmiborthakur/
https://www.facebook.com/profile.
php?id=100069359388049

INSTAGRAM
https://www.instagram.com/poetessmalakshmi/

E-MAIL ID
poetessmalakshmi@gmail.com

Black Eagle Books

www.blackeaglebooks.org
info@blackeaglebooks.org

Black Eagle Books, an independent publisher, was founded
as a nonprofit organization in April, 2019. It is our mission
to connect and engage the Indian diaspora and the world at
large with the best of works of world literature published on a
collaborative platform, with special emphasis on
foregrounding Contemporary Classics and New Writing.

Lightning Source UK Ltd.
Milton Keynes UK
UKHW012359231222
414383UK00006B/411

9 781645 600886